The Soul of the Ozarks

The Paintings & Process of Madison Woods
featuring the
Wild Ozark pigments

Volume I
2023

Introduction

My name is Madison Woods, amateur naturalist, nature-lover, and artist of Wild Ozark. I live with my husband, two horses and a cat in the middle of 160 acres of mostly wild land in the Ozark Mountains of northwest Arkansas. Our nearest town has a population of about 500. Neighbors here are sometimes hundreds of acres apart from each other. We are six miles down a dirt road away from pavement.

What kinds of things does a person want to know about me? Is that my real name? No. I began using that name as a business name, but liked it enough to just adopt it as my alter-ego when people started calling me that. My age? Old enough. Married to the man of my dreams, mother to three incredible people, offspring of a couple of pretty interesting folks, and sister to another.

I'm constantly walking around with one foot in the real world.

The other foot? Mired in the muck of some other plane of existence.

Yes, I'm pretty woo-woo. But I'm also pretty grounded. My entire career history before starting my own business took place in organic, inorganic, and environmental laboratories. If you ask me, this makes me both practical **and** open to worlds that may not exist for other people who walk with both feet "on the ground".

I am fascinated with nature. Nature is my muse. It's the juxtaposition of beauty and brutality that gets me. Liminal spaces… situations… maybe they're just moments in time? I don't know, but they beckon me with a siren's call, and I don't even know how to define them.

When I'm not simultaneously creating (my art) and destroying (my studio/office), I'm either helping Mr. Wild Ozark on our homestead chores, working in the garden, writing or wandering around outside picking up rocks, or in the woods working with the ginseng nursery.

My art is deeply influenced by my life in the remote Ozark Mountains. My paintings are meant to promote a love for Nature, offer a connection to the seemingly brutal circle of life, and I want them to stimulate an awakening to the incredible range of colors in our land (and across the globe!).

Every paint and painting I make instills a sense of awe in me, and I hope that does the same for you.

Other Notes

All of the paintings featured between these pages are currently available. That may change by the time you're reading this, though. You can always see what's for sale and make purchases of originals and prints through my website at WildOzark.com. And if you're just interested in my process or life out here at Wild Ozark, I invite you to subscribe to my blog or stop in to visit every so often. If you join my newsletter subscription, you'll get a free 5 x 7" print and have the chance to enter each month for another one.

Artist Statement

My art is a partnership with the land, and begins with foraging for pigments. I work with the very soul of the Ozarks: ocher rich stones, naturally pigmented clay, soot from the chimney, and charred bone for my earthy colors. While the subjects I paint are varied wildlife and landscapes, the limited palette of earthy colors lends a cohesiveness to my portfolio and a distinctive voice to my body of work, regardless of the focus of the painting. My art is intended to offer patrons an intimate communion with the most ancient of elements that make up our earthly abode.

Contact Information

@wildozark

madison@wildozark.com

wildozark.com

The Colors I Use

You'll notice that my palette is an earthy one. That's because almost all of the colors came from the very earth beneath my feet. The rocks here in the Ozarks where I live are mostly sandstone rocks. There is also some shale, dark gray that lives in the creeks. It is buttery smooth and full of stinky sulfates if I don't wash the pigment before making the paint. And there's another shale of a different composition that lives in the hills and offers a yellowish-tan color. Limestone offers a white, if I can find the chunks that are clean and not stained with iron. But the sandstones are where the reds, russets, yellows, browns, and a sort of green comes from.

After the rocks, there are bones and antlers, and grapevines, too. Those three things give a deep velvet black if I char them before making the paint.

A couple of plants make their way onto my palette sometimes too. Almost all of the plant pigments fade fairly quickly. But the blue juice from the petals of Asiatic dayflower makes a powerful blue stain. And the outer bark of the Osage tree roots give an orange with incredible vibrance and excellent staying power.

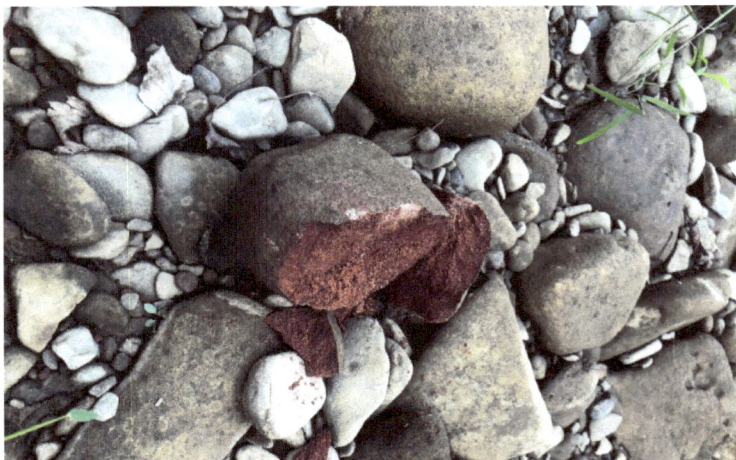

The inside of this sandstone reveals a treasure for a paint-maker.

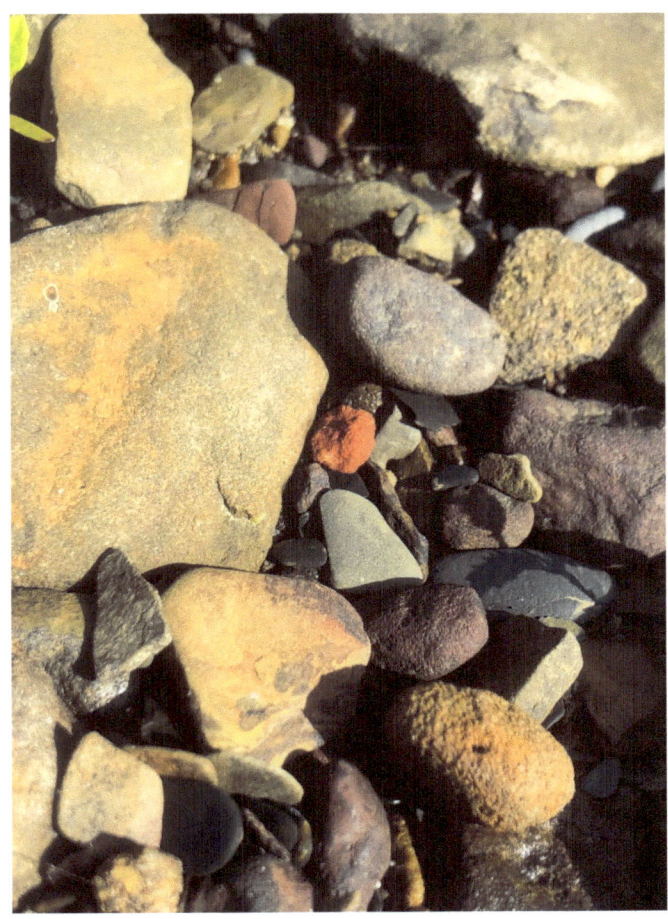

Lots of colors here to choose from.

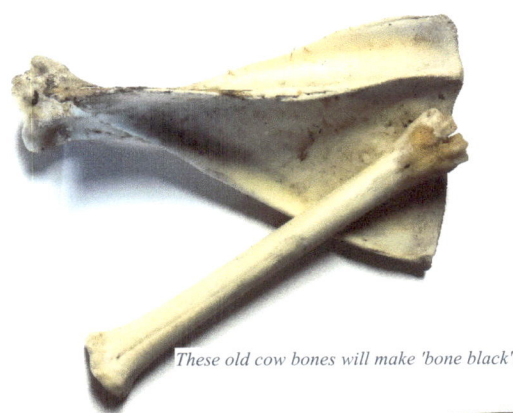

These old cow bones will make 'bone black'.

DESTINATION UNKNOWN

- Size: 20 x 16″
- Media: handmade watercolor, Ozark foraged pigments
- Substrate: watercolor paper
- Pigment source: sandstones (red, russet, brown, yellow), green siltstone, shale, limestone, char

This painting has made the journey to New York City twice so far. It won the Silver Medal of Honor in Aquamedia in the 2020 Audubon Artists' Exhibition at the Salmagundi Club on 5th Ave. Most recently (2023) it traveled again to that neck of the woods to hang in the Re-Imagining Conservation Exhibit by Creature Conserve at the Swale House on Governor's Island.

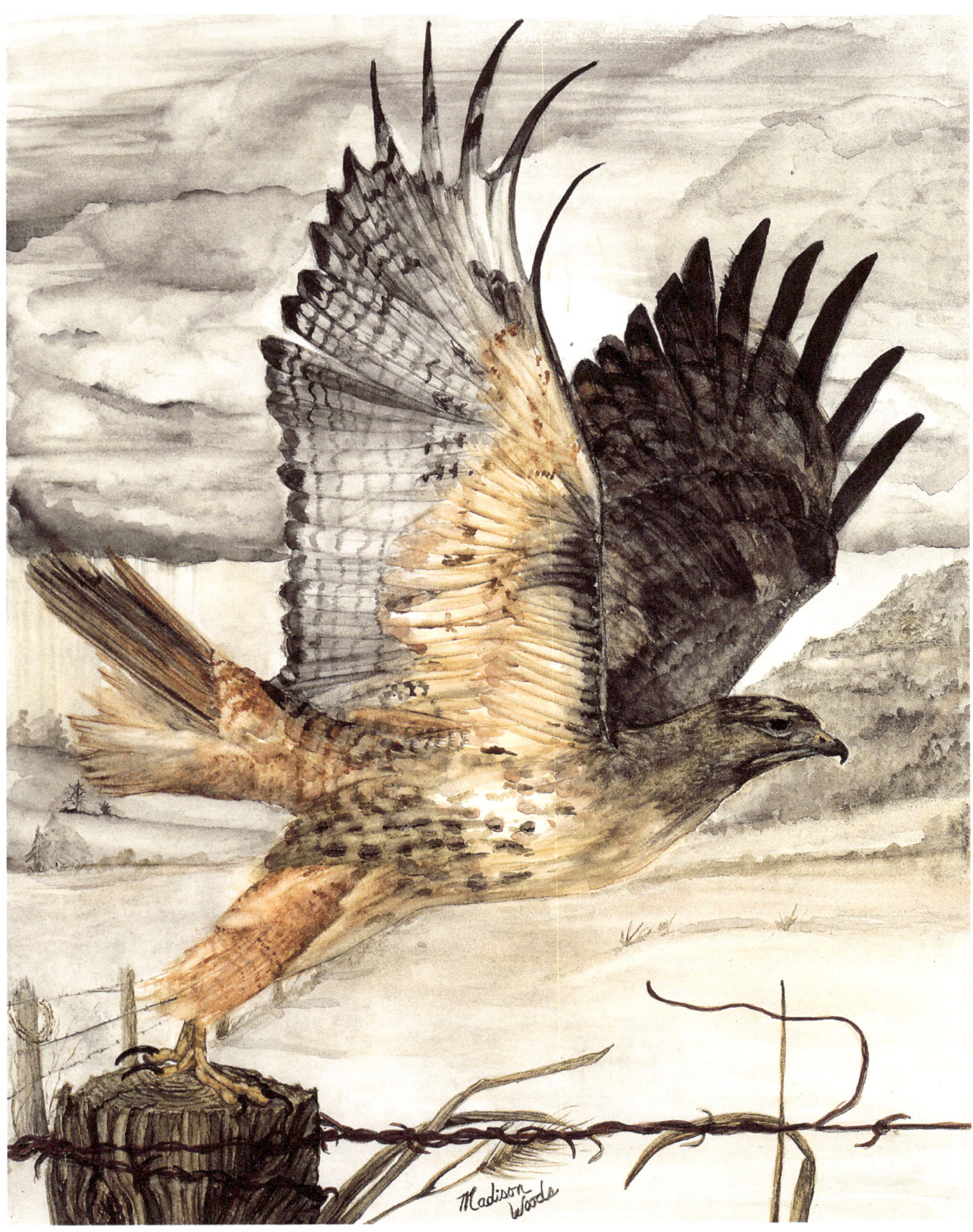

Don't Mess With Me

- Size: 20 x 16"
- Media: handmade watercolor, Ozark foraged pigments
- Substrate: watercolor paper
- Pigment source: sandstones (red, russet, brown, yellow), green siltstone, shale, limestone, Osage root bark

The bark of an Osage tree is a brilliant orange and the pigment is very lightfast. Ordinarily I won't use plant pigments to make my paints, because they inevitably will fade or discolor. Not so with this one. I happily gather the bark of any Osage tree I find down with roots exposed. I watched this one for a full year as it weathered in the middle of a creek down our dirt road. When the color remained true month after month in full sun, I decided to wade out there and collect some of it for experimenting. What resulted was a paint that has now become one of my favorite colors.

About the title. This bald eagle has a defensive posture. She is most likely defending her space on the branch or her position in the hierarchy of her community.

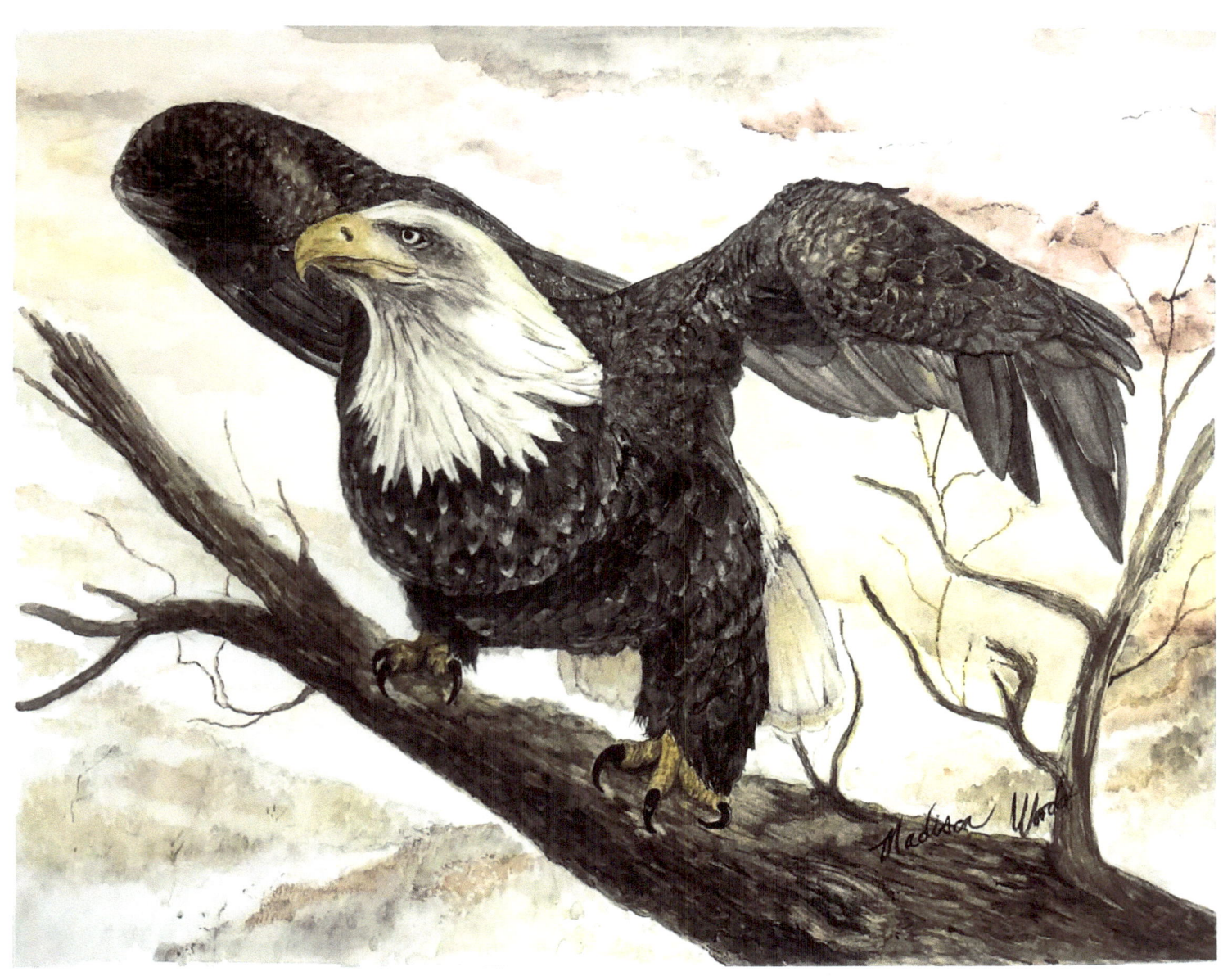

- Size: 5 x 7"
- Media: handmade watercolor, Ozark foraged pigments
- Substrate: handmade paper
- Pigment source: sandstones (red, russet, brown, yellow), green siltstone, shale, limestone, char

Each of my Twisted Trees gain their form and personalities as the painting progresses. When I start one, I don't have a clear idea yet of how it will turn out. Some take on more masculine forms, some obviously feminine, like this one. And some are otherworldly and strange.

Four of Wands shows a mother, fiercely guarding a clutch of eggs that appear to be smooth river stones. It represents dedication to family and society, and willingness to stand firm even through the darkest hours of duress.

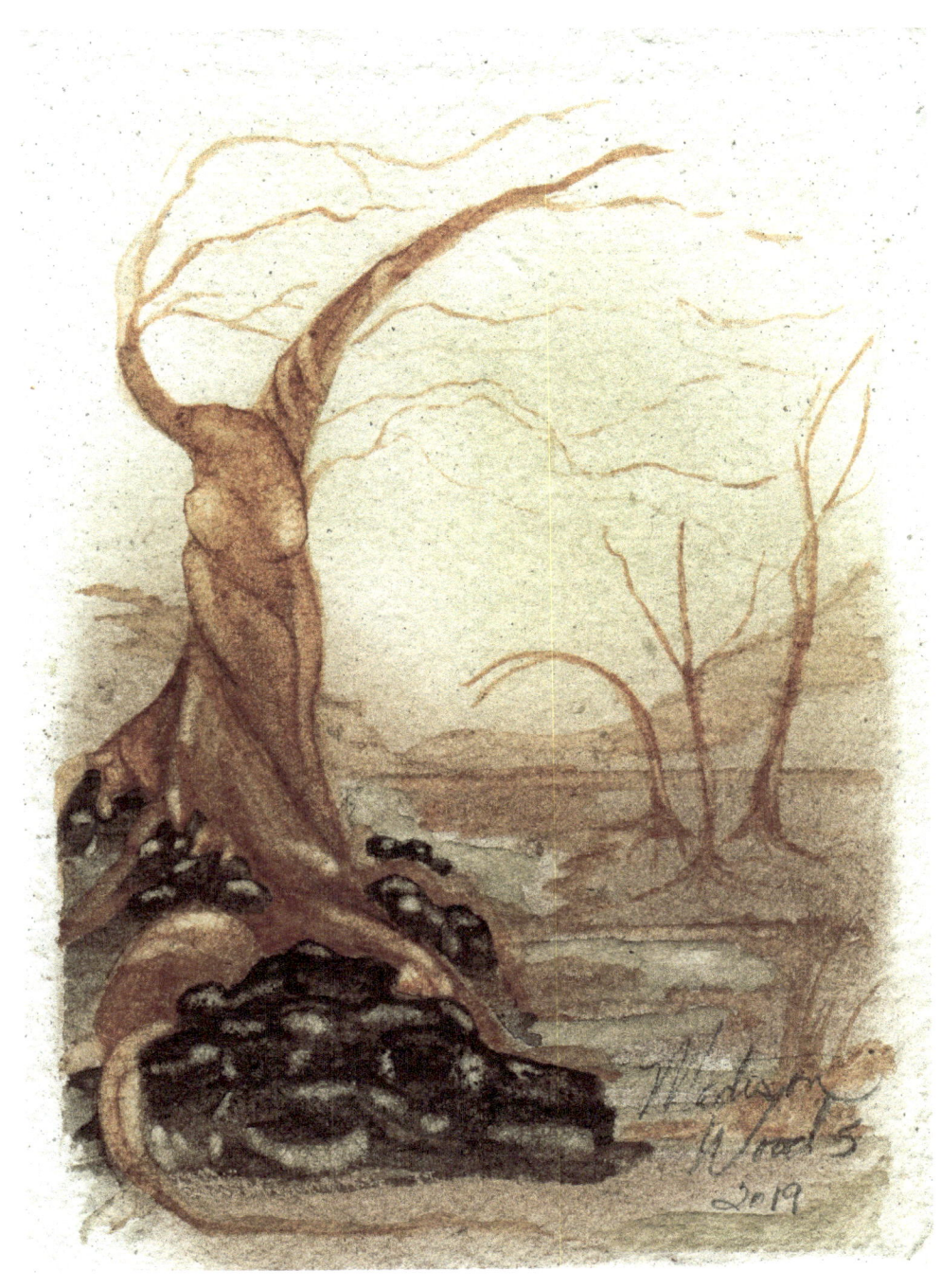

The Process

Most of the rocks I use are easy to find. They're everywhere on our land, on the driveway, or in the creeks. When I walk to the shed to get hay for the horses, I often see a brightly colored piece of hematite in my path. These are usually small, about the size of my thumbnail and fairly flat. I'll put that in my pocket and continue on to finishing the task for the horses.

When I walk my morning mile, it's hard to resist collecting more rocks. Often I can't resist, and so my pockets are full by the time I return to the house. Other times, I put the rocks I find in a little pile on the side of the driveway to come back to later.

And sometimes I go to the creek, specifically to look for good pigment rocks. Wet rocks, when scraped on larger rocks, make an artwork of their own, a mandala sort of work that washes away in the next rain.

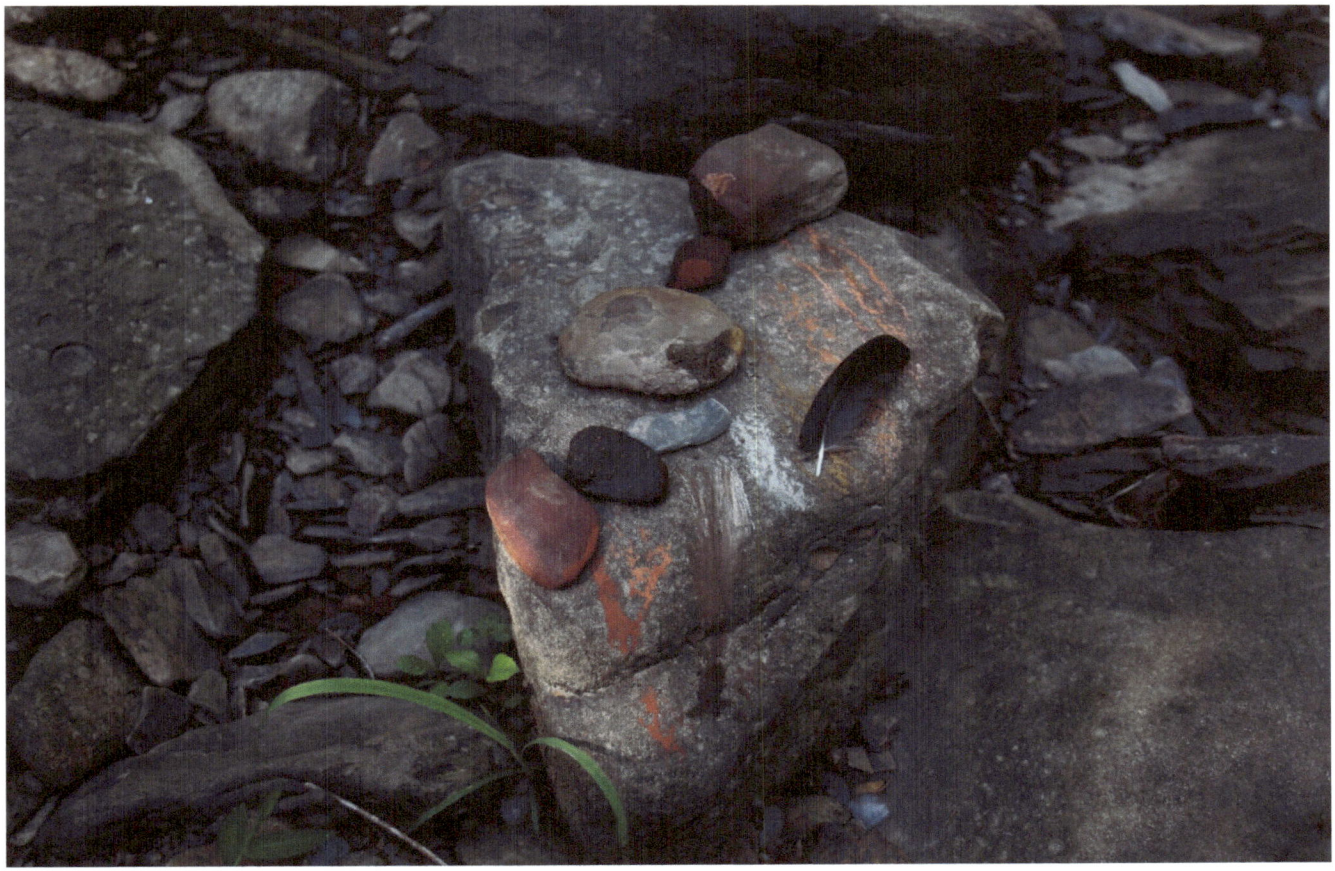

Scraping them like this helps me to judge the quality of the color I might get after making the paint. But the vibrant reds rarely look so red when I'm done. Every color carries an earthy tint with it, and the reds are more rusty; the yellows more umber. At least when I'm making watercolor paints. There is still enough variation between shades to make incredible art. Once I bring the rocks home, I crush them and wash the powders. Then when the powders are dry, I add them to a binder made of gum Arabic, honey, and our spring's water to make watercolor paints. And when the paint is dry, I get to work making a painting.

A Curious Pair

- Size: 14 x 11″
- Media: handmade watercolor, Ozark foraged pigments
- Substrate: cold-pressed watercolor paper
- Pigment source: sandstones (red, russet, brown, yellow), green siltstone, shale, limestone

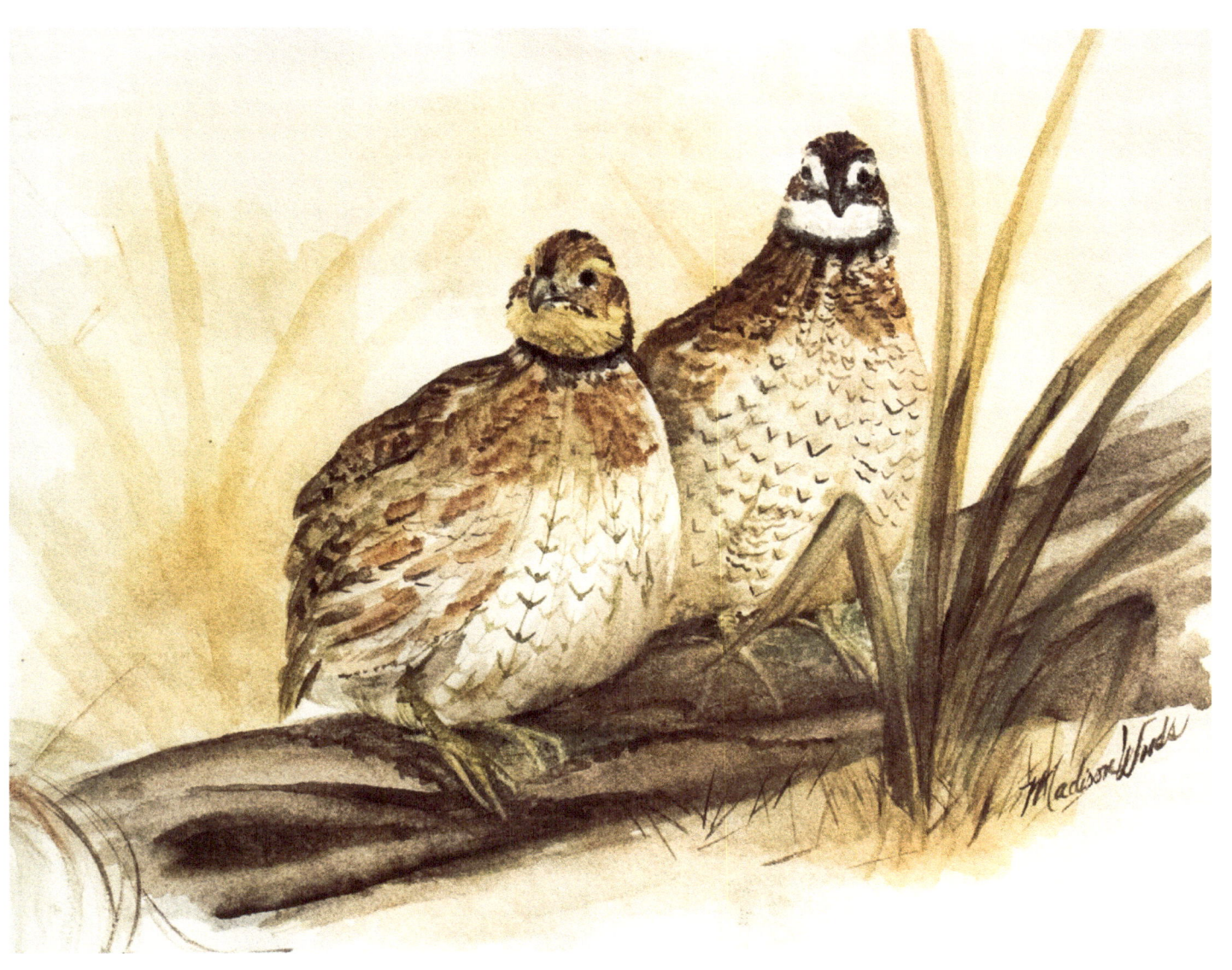

- Size: 16 x 12″
- Media: handmade watercolor, Ozark foraged pigments
- Substrate: watercolor paper
- Pigment source: sandstones (red, russet, brown, yellow), green siltstone, shale, limestone, Osage root bark

This old tractor once belonged to my grandfather, a Cajun man to the core. He used it for farming the rich soils of south Louisiana where I was raised. Eventually my dad became the owner, and he brought it up here to me in northwest Arkansas. Right now it's little more than a relic, albeit a photogenic reminder of days gone by. Eventually I'd love to restore it and put it back to work.

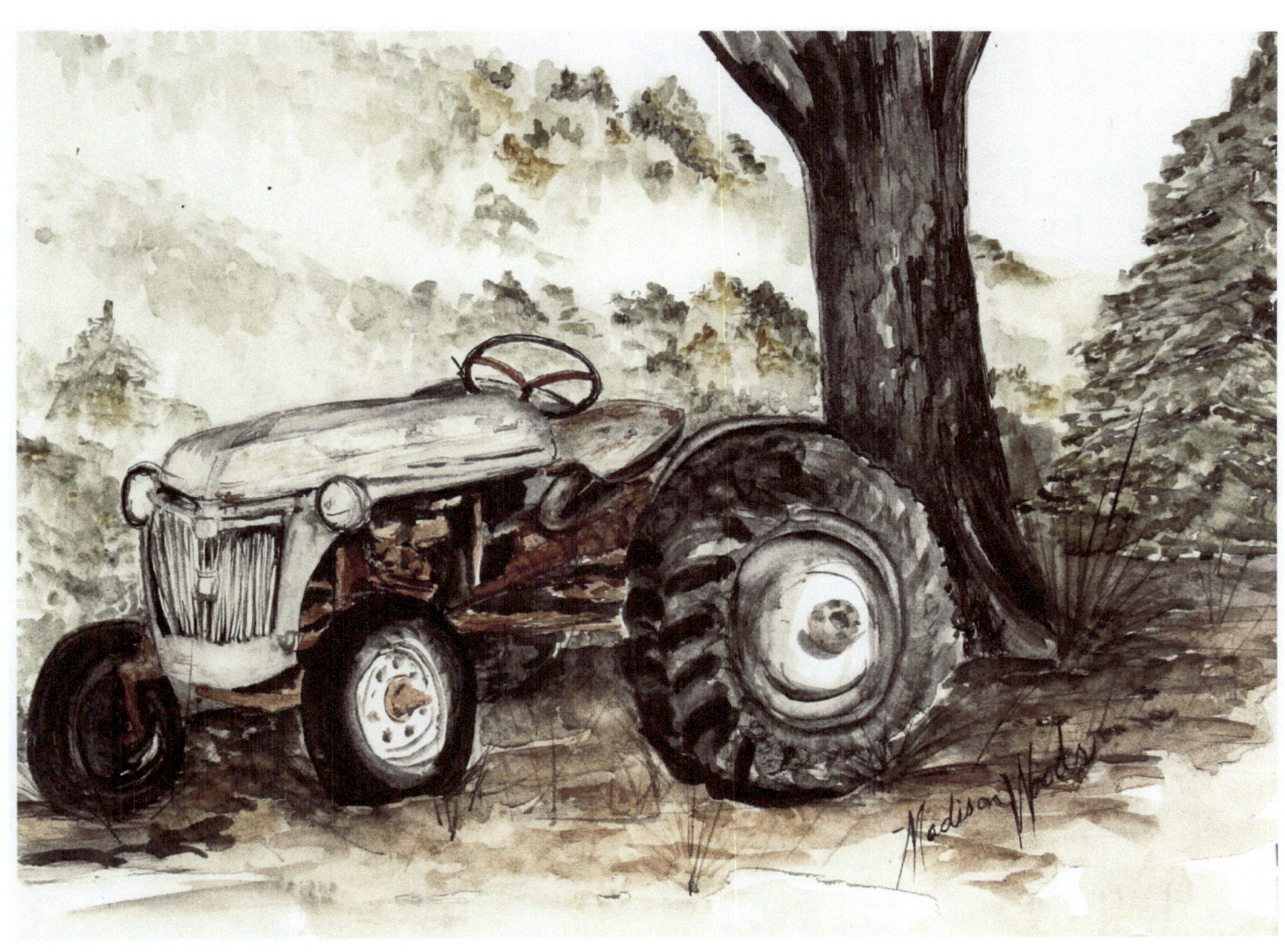

Raccoon on the Rocks

- Size: 12 x 16"
- Media: handmade watercolor, Ozark foraged pigments
- Substrate: black acid-free paper
- Pigment source: sandstones (red, russet, brown, yellow), green siltstone, shale, limestone

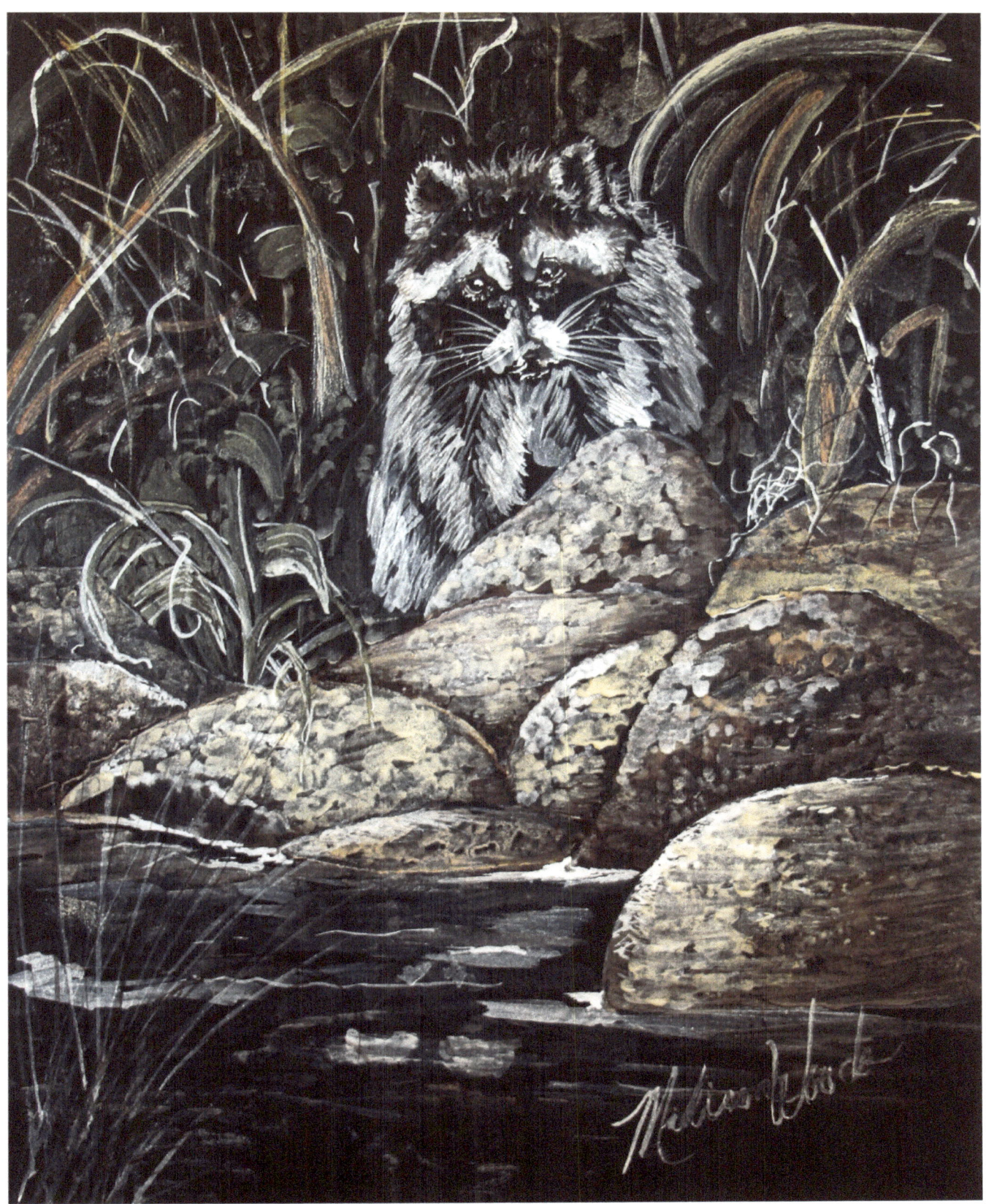

WHISPER

- Size: 30 x 22″
- Media: handmade watercolor, Ozark foraged pigments
- Substrate: watercolor paper
- Pigment source: charred and ashed found/foraged cow bones

This is my largest watercolor painting. It is painted entirely in bone pigments from bleached foraged cow bones that I found. The cow itself is a young heifer that belongs to my granddaughter, who shows her in the county fairs. There is something (or maybe several things) about Brahman cows that I love – the velvet dewlaps and floppy ears, and expressive eyes.

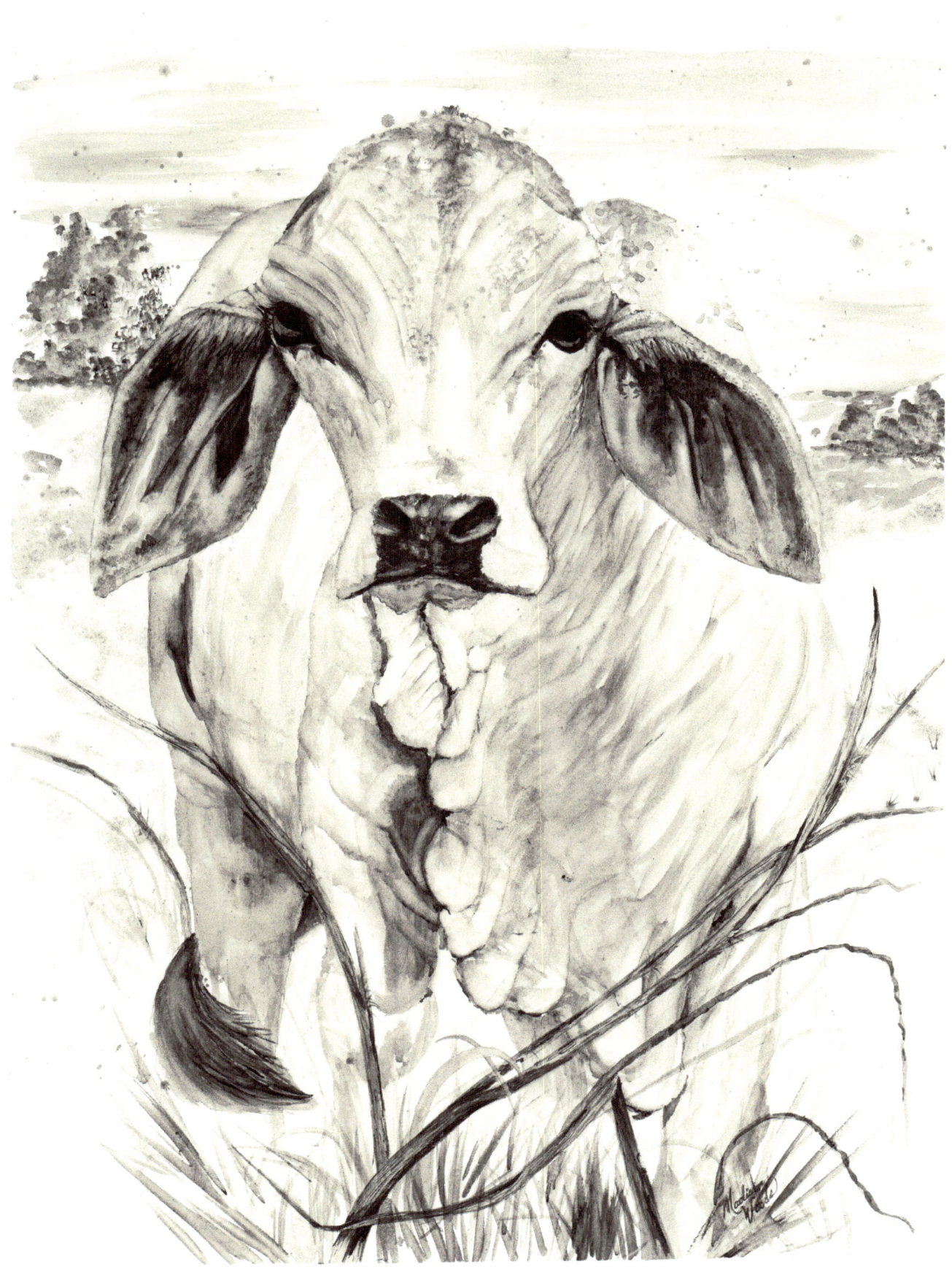

Hay Loft Doors

- Size: 6 x 4"
- Media: handmade watercolor, Ozark foraged pigments
- Substrate: watercolor paper permanently mounted to birch cradle board, varnished and framed in barnwood
- Pigment source: sandstones (red, russet, brown, black), shale

This painting is on watercolor paper permanently mounted onto birch and varnished. It does not need glazing because the varnish protects it from UV and environmental influences. Once I learned the technique of varnishing my watercolors, I rarely felt the desire to put any of them behind glass again.

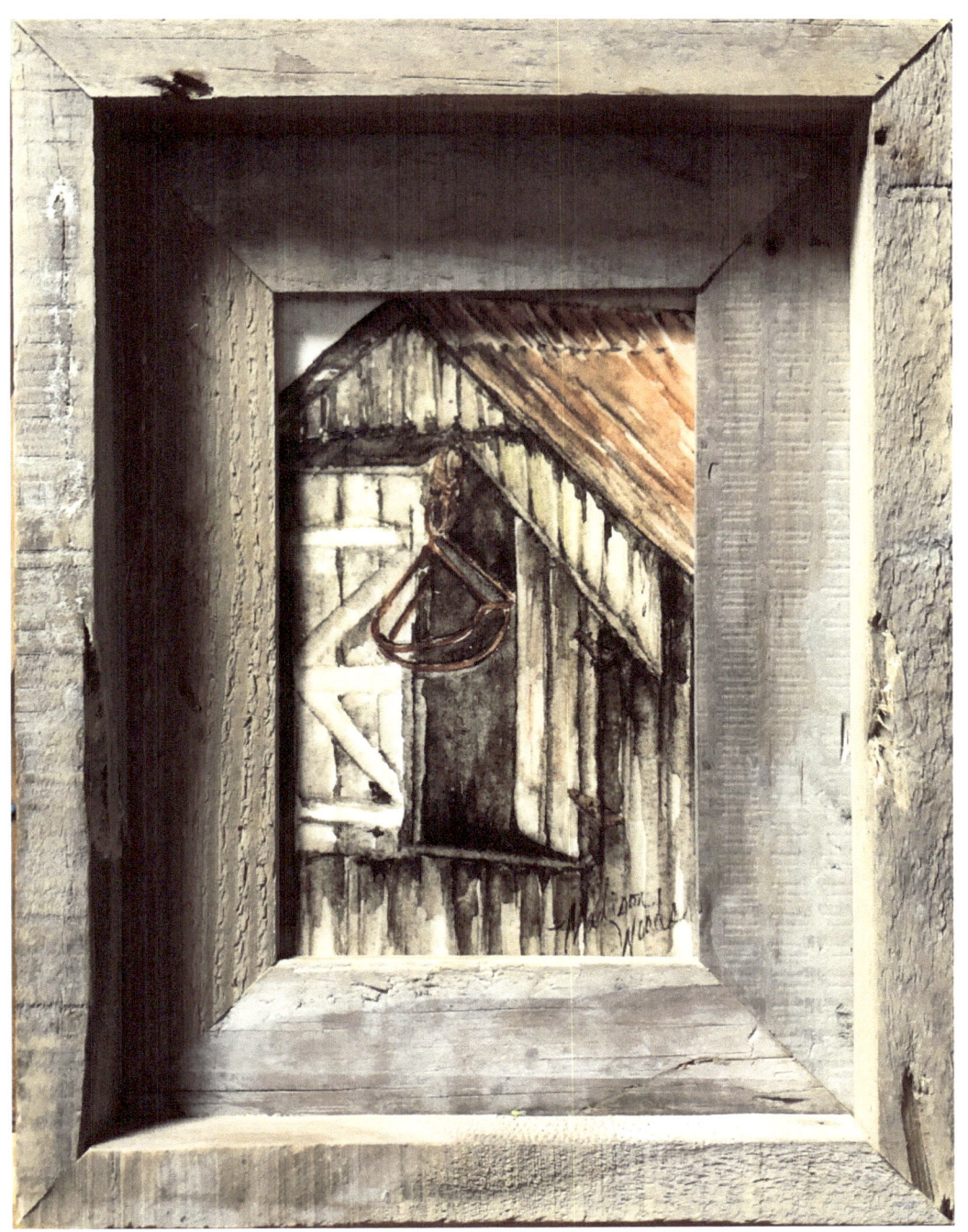

Dr. Carter's Office

- Size: 12 x 16″
- Media: handmade watercolor, Ozark foraged pigments
- Substrate: watercolor paper
- Pigment source: sandstones (red, russet, brown, black yellow), green siltstone, shale, limestone, Osage root bark, Asiatic dayflower petals

Very occasionally, I'll use a plant-sourced pigment. In this painting, the blue came from the petals of Asiatic dayflowers. Before indigo was discovered, the Japanese developed a technique of using the blue juice of these incredibly pigmented flowers. You can't make a 'paint' from it because anything added to the juice causes the molecular structure of the pigment to change and you'll lose the blue. But you can soak a paper with the juice to store it. Once the paper dries, then it can be rewetted with the paint brush. Transfer the dye to the paper and there's the blue. It's a fairly stable color as far as plant pigments go. If kept out of the light, it may last decades. My test samples are still strongly blue, and the color hasn't faded in this painting in the years since I painted it. But it's not permanent in the same way the ochres and earth pigments are.

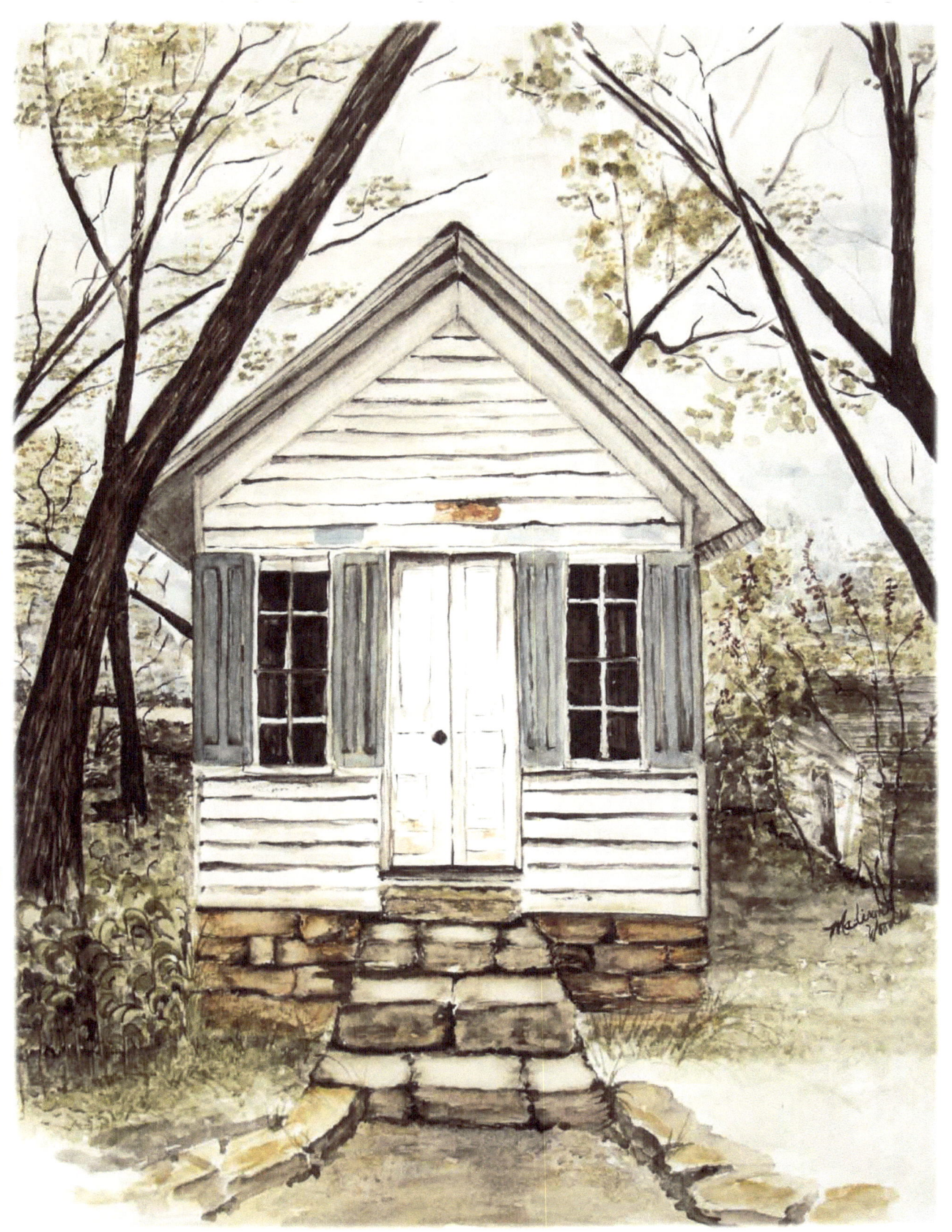

RAIN CROW (YELLOW BILLED CUCKOO)

- Size: 6 x 4″
- Media: handmade watercolor, Ozark foraged pigments
- Substrate: watercolor paper permanently mounted and varnished
- Pigment source: sandstones (brown, yellow), green siltstone, shale

Rain Crows are one of the often heard, but seldom seen birds that live out here. I love the tropical, staccato sounds of their calls, which only begin once the days are hot and sultry. While their reproductive habits are disturbing, because the female puts her eggs in the nests of other birds, which displaces the original chicks, I still look forward to hearing the sounds and seeing glimpses of the Cuckoo flying through the woods.

This painting is permanently mounted onto a birch cradleboard, varnished, and framed in barnwood. The varnish is archival and protects from UV and environmental damage. No glass is needed.

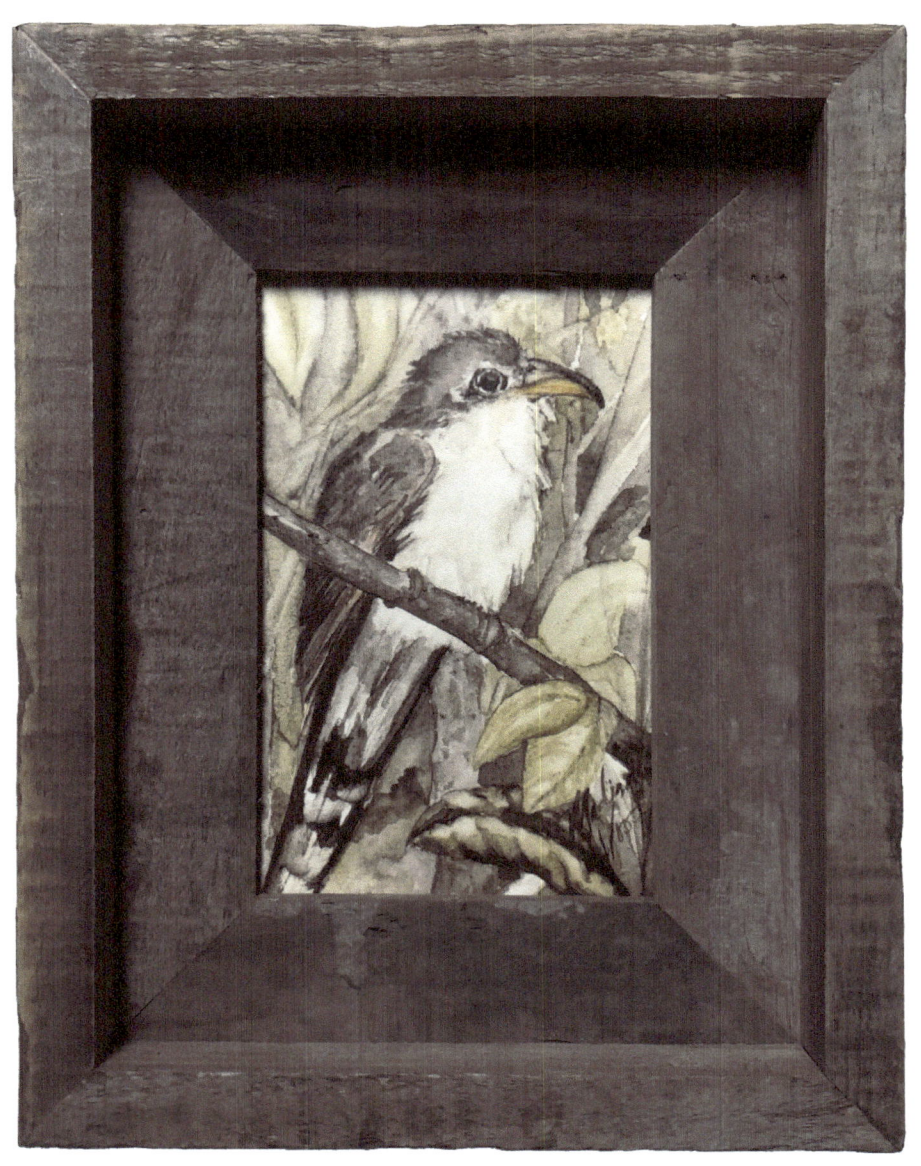

Discovering Oils

A New Adventure

Near the end of October 2022, I decided to make a few tubes of oil paints. Until this time, I'd only made watercolor paints. With the test paints, I made three small test paintings. Mainly I wanted to know if I would even like using oil paints. The first paintings were crude, because the paints themselves were pretty crude and hastily made.

Previously during the week on one of my morning mile walks, I'd taken photos of a few different kinds of mushrooms I'd found. Those were the subjects of my first attempts to paint with Ozark pigments in oils.

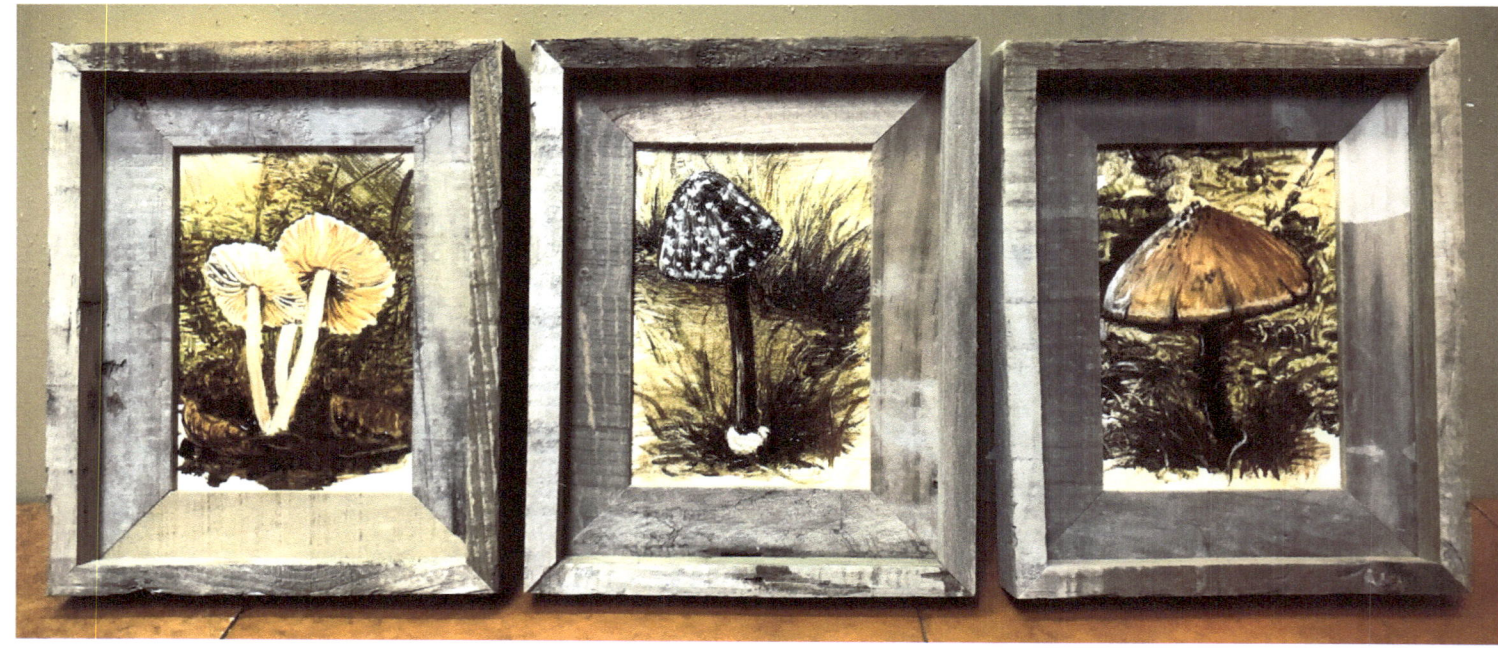

My little experiment was enough to inform me about the challenges, and the rewards, of working with oils and these earthy wild Ozark pigments. At that time, though, I had several commissions lined up for watercolor paintings, and so I put the oil paints aside. Once the commissions were out of the way, my plan was to devote all of my effort to making better oil paints, and to learn how to make them behave as desired on the canvas.

When I received an offer to buy those three little mushroom paintings, the sale cemented my commitment to pursue this new and exciting path.

A Local, Sustainable Art

With watercolors, all of the ingredients I use are locally sourced except for the gum Arabic. I looked into using other gums that do occur locally but didn't have good results with them. So I resigned to outsourcing the gum. One reason it took me so long to try making oil paints is that I was afraid I'd have to outsource too much.

When I began research into drying oils, though, a large part of my fear was alleviated. Walnut oil is a drying oil that can be used for oil painting. We have a lot of black walnut trees on our property and if I needed to, I could produce my own black walnut oil. A small press for expelling the oil is necessary to make it, but it's not so large an investment that I can't get one eventually. All I absolutely need for the oil paints are my pigments and some oil. There are other oil sources I can grow, including sunflowers and linseed (flax). Perilla is a weed here that produces copious seeds, and it, too, is a drying oil. So I have options with oils.

The two things I outsource for the oil paints are turpentine (which, again, I could make if I had to) and titanium dioxide powder. When I clean my brushes I use the turpentine, and it's the only 'chemical' I use in my process. I use oils to thin the paints where necessary. The titanium gives me white paint. I've tried our local resources and there is nothing that makes an opaque white color, a necessary thing in order to give my pigments a variety of values.

Before starting an oil painting, the surface needs to be primed. I do buy the gesso, but this, too, is something I could make using rabbit skin glue and limestone powder. There's a ready supply of both rabbits and limestone here. I made a batch of it once, just to be sure it could be done, and sure enough it can. However, while I have the funds to purchase this, I will.

With oil paintings, I don't need paper. I can paint on any surface that allows it, but I prefer to paint on ¼" plywood boards. While I can't source plywood on my own, my husband has a sawmill and a planer, so he could at least plane some boards to a workable thickness (or rather, thin-ness) for me if necessary. We have an abundant source of hardwoods I could use.

Paint brushes are on my list of things to learn how to make. At the moment, I am buying those, and all of the squirrels in the woods are hoping that I don't get started too soon on that project. I did gather some horse's tail hair when I trimmed last, to see how that works for a brush one day, though. I think I could make a serviceable brush if I had to.

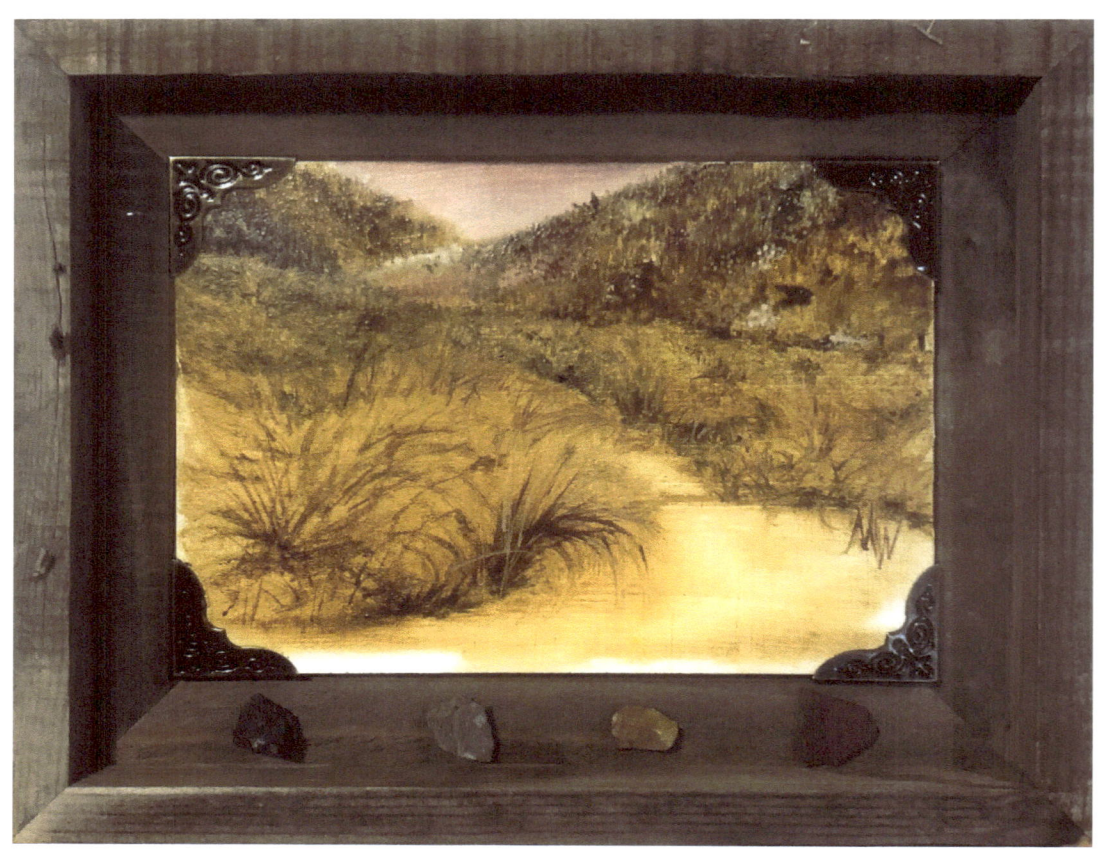

Plum Blossoms and Redbuds on the Mountains. I enjoy framing in creative, non-conventional ways. This is a 5 x 7" oil painting on birch plywood with metal corners, top-mounted on a barnwood frame. The rocks are samples of the same ones that made the paints that I used.

Making Oil Paints

The process for making my oil paints is the same as for making watercolors up until the point of adding pigment to the binder. First the pigment source is gathered. I use rocks, soot, and bones. Each of these three types of sources have different processing needs. To get smooth paints from the rocks, once they've been broken and ground into dust, I wash them. Shale needs to be washed to get out contaminating water-soluble compounds, and for the same reason so does the chimney soot and bones. Bones need to be charred to black before grinding and washing them.

I bet you're wondering where I get the bones. Believe it or not, they're not hard to come by. Old, weathered bones and antlers turn up fairly often on my hikes and walks. But with our annual deer seasons, it's not hard to gather a stash of bones from meals and put them outside to weather in a more convenient location.

The paintings on the following pages are my favorite ones that I've completed through June of 2023. I hope you enjoy them as much as I enjoyed creating them.

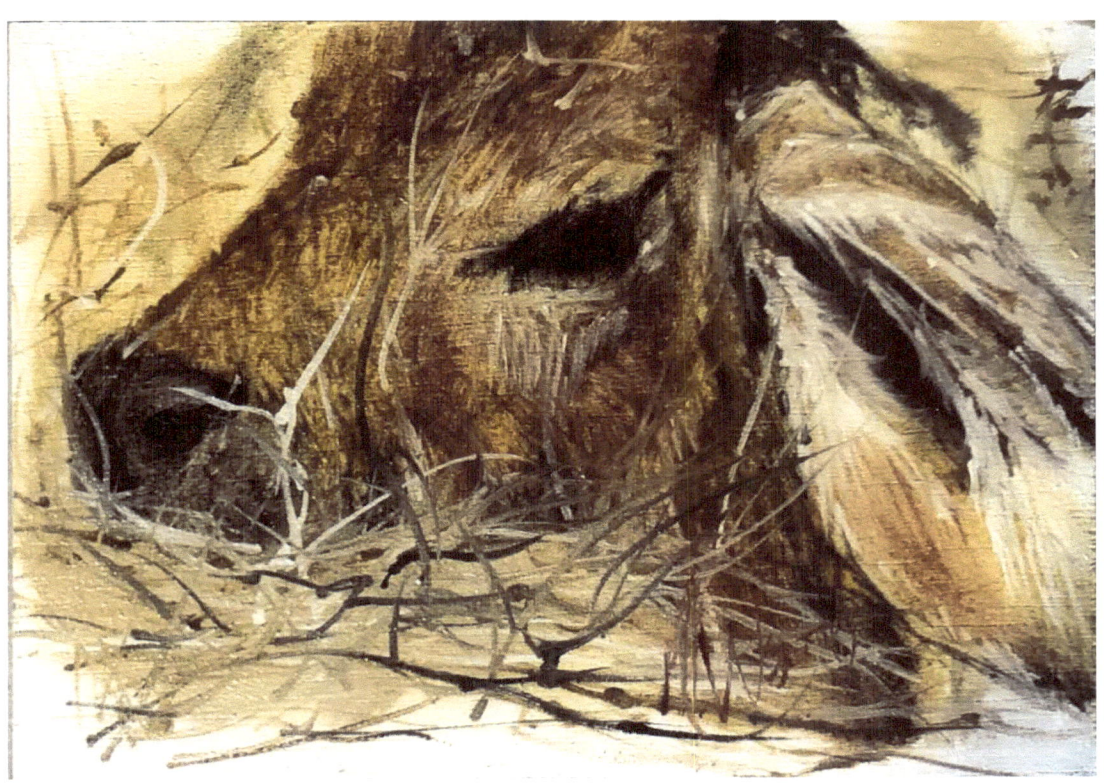

- Size: 16 x 20″
- Media: handmade oils, Ozark foraged pigments
- Substrate: birch cradle board
- Pigment source: sandstones (red, russet, brown, yellow), green siltstone, shale, limestone, bone, and titanium

Wild Ozark's 160 acres is part of the Kings River Watershed. The little creek that runs through our land gathers its ice-cold waters from springs that emerge in the hollers and hills. It feeds into a larger creek named Felkins, which in turns feeds the Kings River.

There are six low-water bridges on the dirt road that leads to home. When it rains more than an inch or so, these bridges often flood and we are land-locked until it recedes. And every time the torrents wash through the creek and river beds, a new crop of rocks are deposited, and I rejoice.

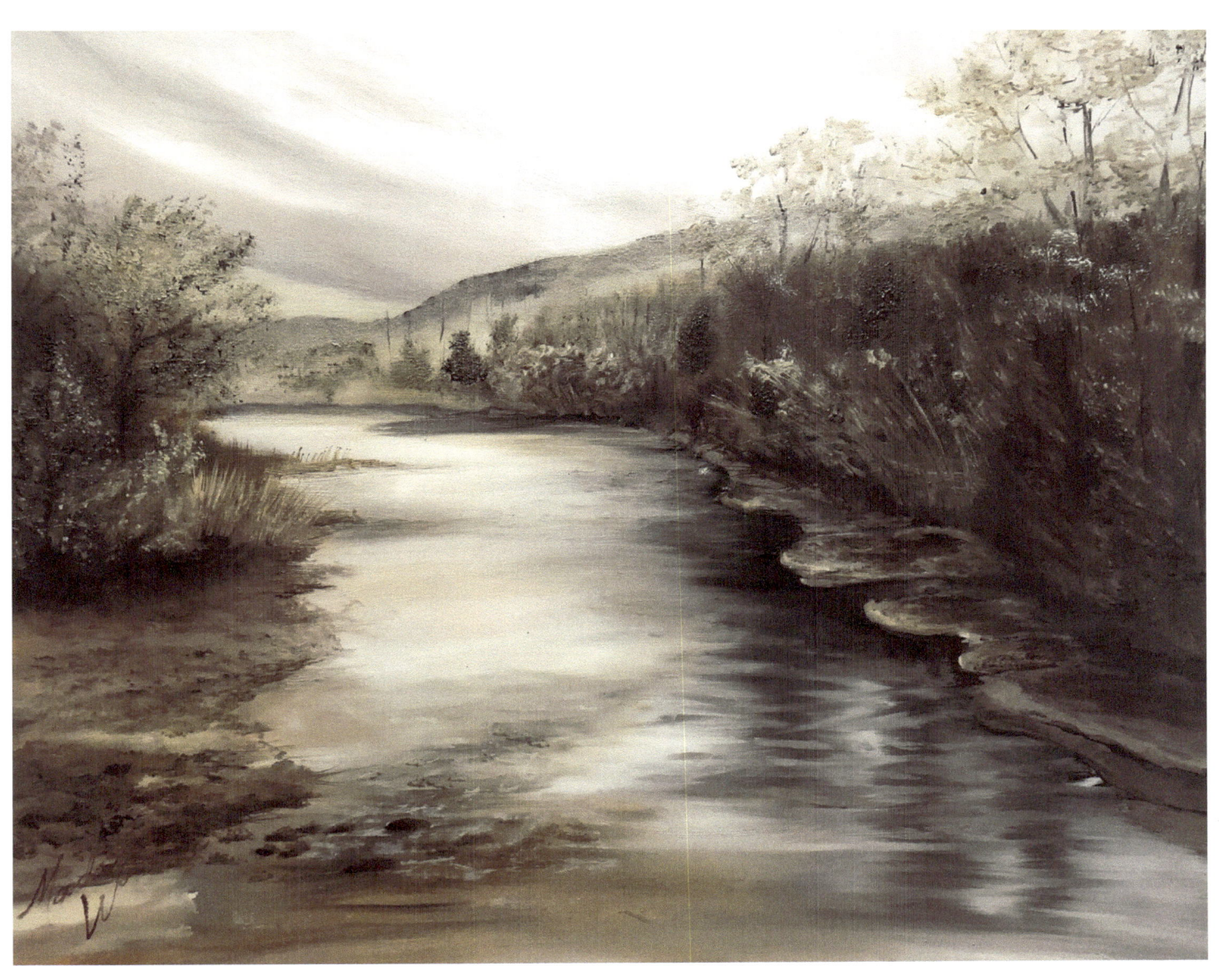

DETOUR FOR A THIRSTY RAVEN

- Size: 37 x 29″
- Media: handmade oils, Ozark foraged pigments
- Substrate: birch ¼″ plywood
- Pigment source: sandstones (red, russet, brown, yellow), green siltstone, shale, limestone, bone, and titanium

This painting embodies the old-world colors so perfectly suited for these earthy Ozark pigments. It's the largest canvas I've worked on as of yet, and was the most enjoyable painting to produce so far. The scene is imaginary, so there was no reference image to work from, though I did look at a lot of pictures of ravens and kegs. Without a guide to what a beer cave or cellar might look like, I made one up. A picture of a raven in that position was nowhere to be found, so I improvised with a stance I thought a raven would possibly take if he wanted to get to the beer flowing from the spigot. The spigot and fittings are all imagined.

I made this painting for a specific exhibit at a local brewery. They liked it so much that it is now featured on the label of their anniversary bottled brew.

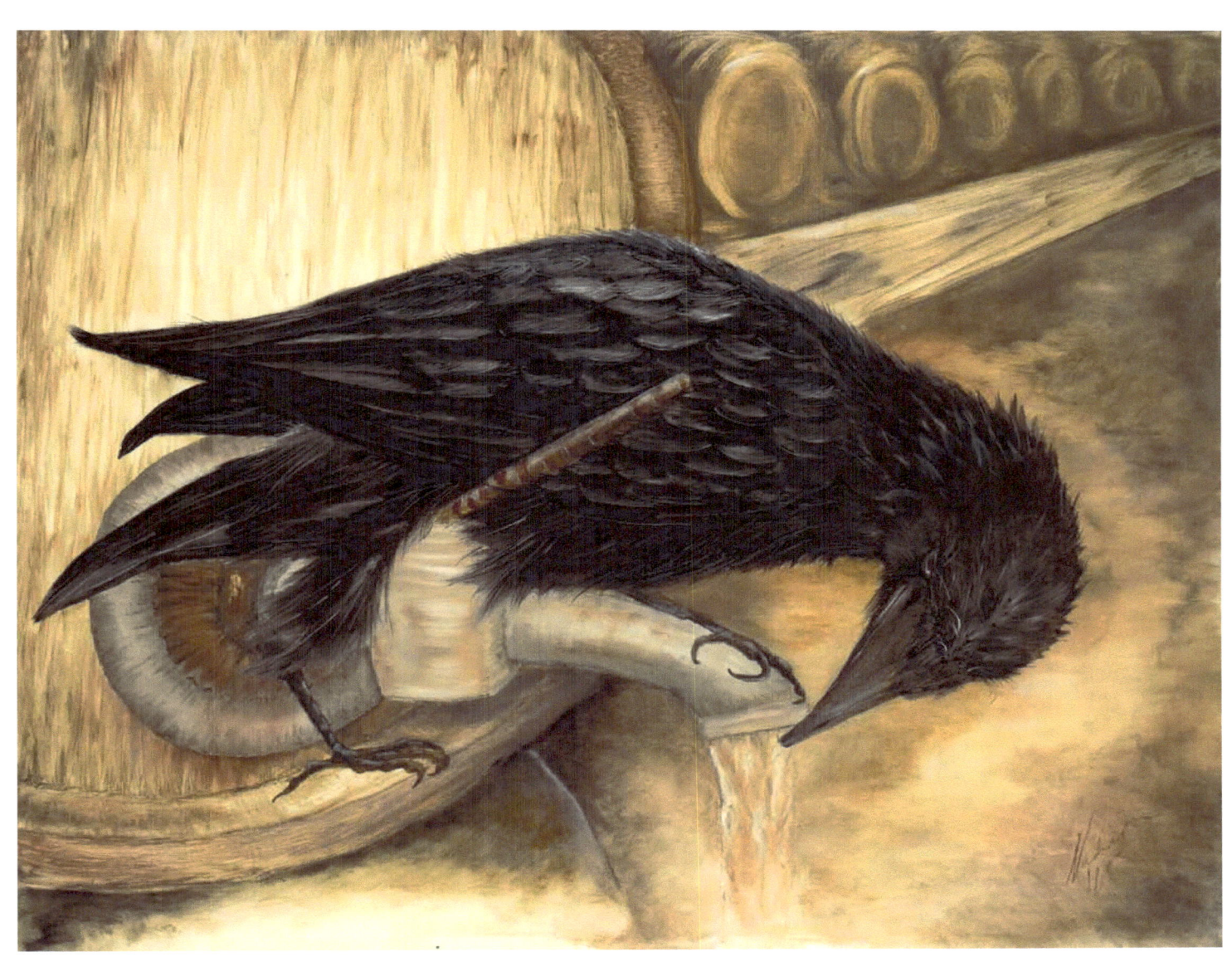

GRUMPY LIL' FELLA

- Size: 12 x 9″
- Media: handmade oils, Ozark foraged pigments
- Substrate: birch cradle board
- Pigment source: sandstones (red, russet, brown, yellow), green siltstone, shale, limestone, bone, and titanium

One year when I came in from work one evening, there were three little screech owls sitting in the grape vines by the gate. I'd been watching their progress as the mother sat in the nest in a hollow tree nearby. The chicks had grown too large for the tiny hole in the tree and they'd finally fledged.

Of course, I didn't have my camera handy, but I drove the rest of the ½ mile to the house and grabbed it anyway. I didn't think they'd still be there when I returned, but they were. This painting is one of the little ones from that day.

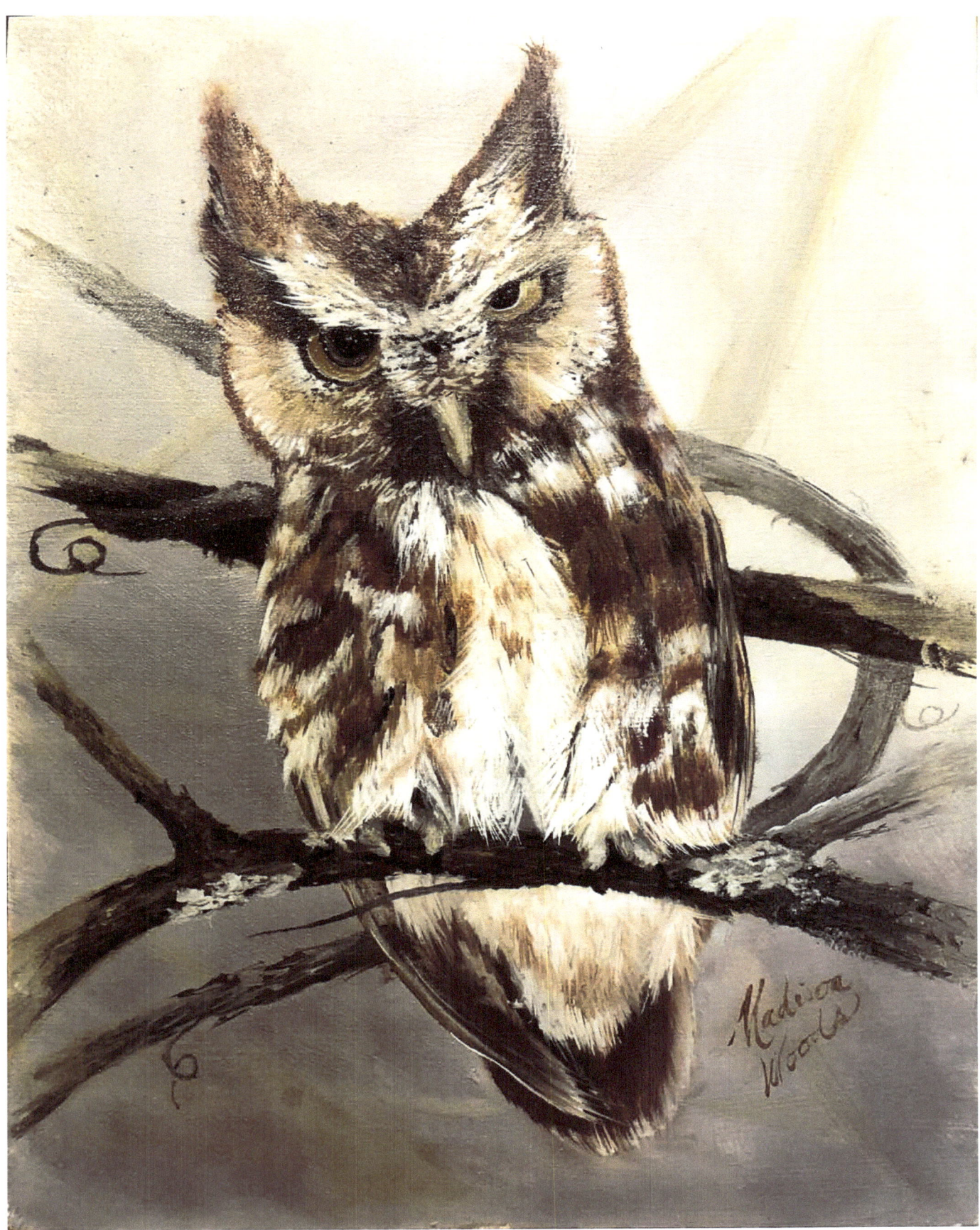

Madison Woods

I'm always interested to see the stages a painting goes through before it is finished. So, I'll share my bad start and messy middles with you, too. This is scary proposition for an artist. It lays bare the reality that not all of us are perfect at what we do (probably none of us are). In the art world, it seems that to share these stages of an artwork is frowned upon. Let me know if this is something you enjoy seeing or if you'd rather not see a work until it's completely finished,

Grumpy Lil' Fella
Progression

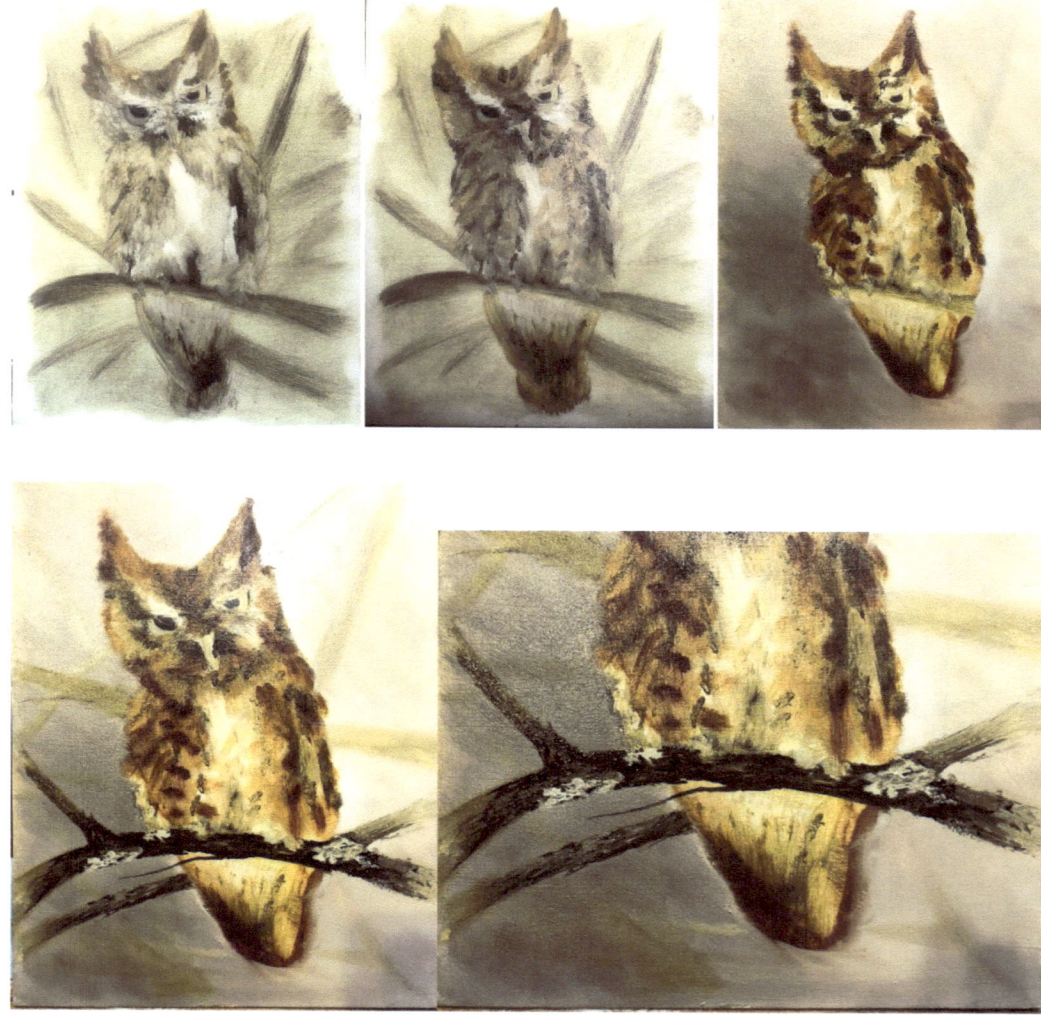

and only then.

More to Come

Going forward I'll continue to improve my techniques for both making paints and making paintings. My production rate averages about one painting a month, with some months resulting in several smaller works.

If you'd like to be notified when I am finished with new paintings, either subscribe to my mailing list and check off the box to be notified of new original works, or watch the 'In Progress' category of my online shop. While I'm working on a painting, or waiting for it to dry, they're placed into that category. Anyone who buys an original while it's in that category will enjoy a discount for the hassle of waiting for me to get it ready to ship.

Thank you for joining me on this journey. If you'd like to know more, I'm happy to take your emails. Just write to me at madison@wildozark.com. I'm always blogging about what I do, and you can find my posts at WildOzark.com anytime!

Until next year's edition,

Yours truly,

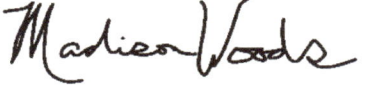

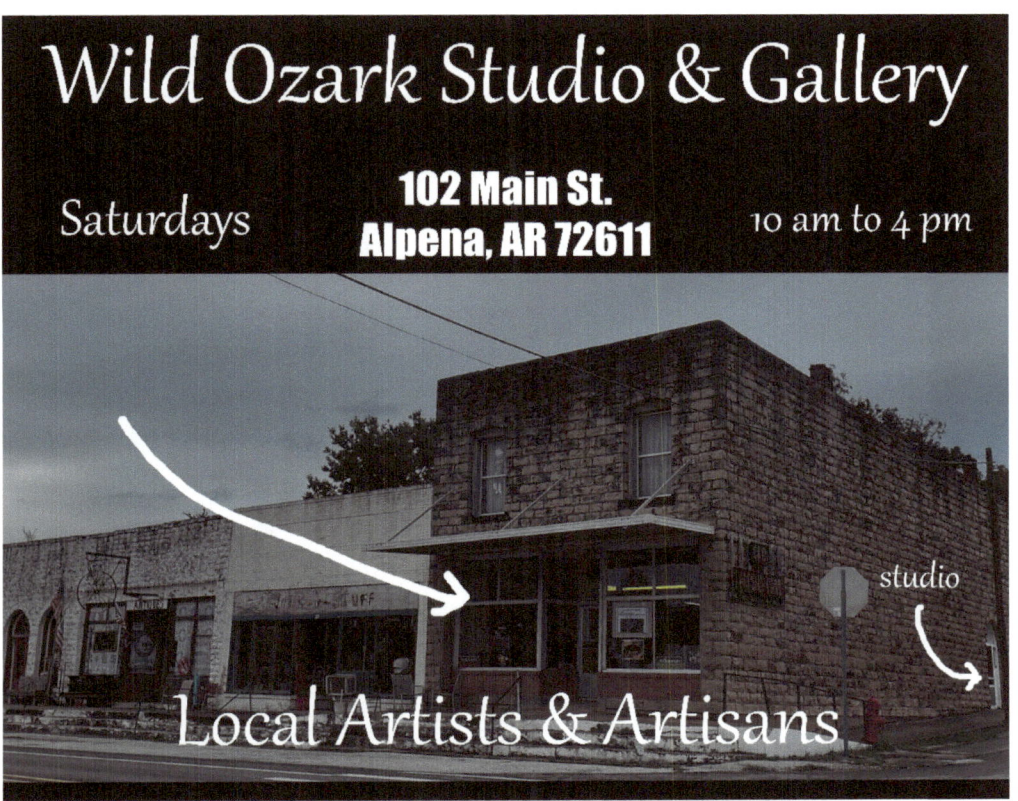

Brought to you by Homegrown Tomatoes LLC

www.ingramcontent.com/pod-product-compliance
Lightning Source LLC
Chambersburg PA
CBHW060838290526
45792CB00006BB/1976